*To My Family*

*Bhaskar*
*Amesh*
*Pravin*
*Sarena*

*To the stars of my life for the peace, love and togetherness that we share now and forever.*

# Preface

The inspiration for creating this unique gourmet cookbook came from the support and encouragement of; my family, friends, students who've participated in my cooking classes and the many who have enjoyed my spice blends and cookbooks.

Creating these recipes has been a loving and fun-filled experience in my kitchen. I recall my mother always saying, "Cooking with a loving heart produces great dishes!"

This book is created to compliment the spices I blend and sell, making it easy for anyone to prepare delicious gourmet dishes.

Enjoy the Symphony of Taste!
Daksha Narsing

# Acknowledgements

To my husband, friend and partner, Bhaskar and my wonderful children Amesh, Pravin and Sarena for their unconditional love and inspiration.

To my mother, for her love and vast knowledge in the art of Indian Cuisine. To my grandmother, for sharing her wisdom in the short time we had together. To my mother-in-law for her love and sharing her way of cooking.

To my dear friend and editor Shelly Peel for her love, patience and true friendship. To Shelly's family, Darcy, Chelsea and Danica for their patience and support.

Last, but not least, to all my friends and students for encouraging me to create another cookbook.

I am grateful to all of these people, without them this book would not have become a reality.

# The Origin

This cuisine originates from the states of Rajestan and Gujarat, in India. My ancestry originates from Rajestan. The recipes and the blending of garam masala, thana jeeroo and chai (tea) masala have been traced back to Rajestan, going back several centuries.

I was born in Northern Rhodesia, Africa where my parents ran a business and raised six children. I have three older sisters and two younger brothers. At the age of eight I lived in India for two years with my sisters in a boarding school in Poona, India. During our school holidays, in India, we would visit our grandparents in Gujarat, where I learned the value of the spices from my grandmother, who was the village herbalist and chiropractor. All of the villagers came to her for treatments for various ailments.

Later I returned to Africa, and learned my mother's style of cooking. I found it was similar to my grandmother's style as my mother had spent many years during her early married life with her mother-in- law. My mother taught me the importance of patiently picking, cleaning, grinding and storing spices.

My family then moved to England during troubled times in Zambia. I lived in England for seven years, until I met my husband Bhaskar and moved to Canada. Once in Canada I learned methods of my mother-in-law's style of cooking.

Celebrated spice combinations and recipes have been handed down in my family throughout the centuries, giving my three wonderful mothers the knowledge they've shared with me. My cookbook is a culmination of my own recipes and those of my ancestors. I am delighted to share these wonderful recipes with you and your family.

# Spices for Healthy Eating

India has a vast range of spices. Spices are used for medicinal purposes, flavor and the preservation of food. The Ayurvedic practices of herbal medicine strongly recommend spices in our daily eating to maintain a healthy body. Ayurvedic medicine suggests that there be a balance of "hot" and "cold" foods and spices in our daily diet. The terms "hot" and "cold" do not refer to temperature or taste, in this case, but rather to the make up of foods.

Hot foods and spices for example, are: meat, chillies, cloves, peppers, cardamom and ginger. Examples of cold foods and spices, on the other hand, are: potatoes, rice, certain beans, cumin, coriander and nutmeg.

Spices are therefore blended in such a way that the mixtures or masalas are balanced. To make the best possible masala or mixture, I pick flavorful, fresh spices and spend many long hours cleaning each spice. When I clean I sift through every seed taking out foreign objects and seeds. The spices are then combined together, using recipes that have been handed down in my family throughout the centuries. The spice blends are then ground and sieved to perfection. Hence, the spice blends are absolutely pure giving the food the best possible taste and the balance needed for a healthy body.

Four spices and three spice mixtures are mainly used in traditional Gujarati cooking, these include: garam masala, thana jeeroo, red chillie powder, turmeric powder, black mustard seeds, whole cumin seeds  and whole spices (cassia sticks, cardamom, black peppercorns,  cloves).  The recipes in this book will use all seven spices and mixtures in various combinations to give you tantalizing and mouthwatering dishes.

All of the spices and mixtures may be purchased from Daksha's Gourmet Spices website, at www.spicesgourmet.com. Most of the spices are also available in your local supermarket, in the ethnic food section, along with some of the flours and lentils mentioned in this cookbook.

# How to Use This Book

This cookbook compliments the spices that are cleaned, blended and sold by Daksha's Gourmet Spices. Buy spices directly from Daksha via the internet at *www. spicesgourmet.com* or e-mail at *daksha@telus.net.* If you prefer, purchase spices from your local supermarket in the ethnic food section.

Prepare ginger/garlic masala (page 82), green chillie masala (page 83) and garlic masala (page 84). These are fresh mixtures, and can be made quickly and easily and stored in the freezer. The ginger/garlic masala and the green chillie masala are used in many recipes in this cookbook. The garlic masala is used mainly for fish dishes.

Refer to the glossary section, starting on page 100, to fully understand Gujarati words and cooking vocabulary. Explore the index provided at the back of this cookbook to find mouthwatering recipes.

Meal Suggestions are included for your convenience, beginning on page 95. But don't be afraid to explore and make your own combinations of meals and remember, have fun cooking!

# *Appetizers*

# Appetizers

# Samosas

## Ground Beef Filling

### Ingredients:

3 lbs ground beef*
1 medium onion diced
4 teaspoons ginger/garlic masala
1 teaspoon green chillie masala
3 teaspoons garam masala
3 teaspoons thana jeeroo
2 teaspoons red chillie powder
1 teaspoon turmeric powder
3 teaspoons salt
12 tablespoons olive oil
3 tablespoons chopped cilantro

### Method:

1. Mix ginger/garlic masala, green chillie masala, garam masala, thana jeeroo, red chillie powder, turmeric powder and salt in 4 tablespoons of olive oil to make a paste.
2. Add paste to ground beef, and blend in the spices. Allow meat to marinate in the refrigerator for approximately 2 hours.
3. Heat 4 tablespoons of olive oil in a pan. Add the marinated beef and stir until meat is browned and separated. Allow to cook on low heat until oil separates and meat is thoroughly cooked.
4. Sauté onions in a separate pan in 4 tablespoons of olive oil.
5. Add sautéd onions and chopped cilantro to the cooked ground beef. Stir. Set aside and allow to cool.

Samosas are an Indian delicacy enjoyed at special occasions. This recipe is concluded on page 18 and is well worth the effort.

*Can be replaced with ground chicken, ground turkey, ground lamb or ground pork meat.

**Continued on next page**

# Samosas cont.

## Vegetable Filling

### Ingredients:

5-6 medium potatoes
1 medium onion chopped
1 cup frozen peas
2 teaspoons ginger/garlic masala
1 teaspoon green chillie masala
1 teaspoon red chillie powder
2 teaspoons thana jeeroo
1 teaspoon turmeric powder
2 teaspoons salt
1 teaspoon cumin seeds
6 tablespoons olive oil
4 tablespoons chopped cilantro

### Method:

1. In a pan heat olive oil and add cumin seeds.
2. Add chopped onions. Sauté till onions are lightly browned.
3. Wash frozen peas and drain in warm water. Add diced potatoes, ginger/garlic masala, green chillie masala, thana jeeroo, red chillie powder, turmeric powder and salt and stir well.
4. Cover and allow to cook on low heat for about 20 to 30 minutes, stirring occasionally till vegetables are thoroughly cooked.
5. Garnish with chopped cilantro and set aside to cool.

**Continued on next page**

# Samosas cont.

## Chicken Filling

### Ingredients:

2 cups cubed chicken breast
1 onion chopped
2 medium potatoes
3 teaspoons ginger/garlic masala
3 teaspoons garam masala
3 teaspoons thana jeeroo
1 teaspoon red chillie powder
1 teaspoon turmeric powder
3 teaspoons salt
8 tablespoons olive oil

### Method:

1. Mix ginger/garlic masala, garam masala, thana jeeroo, red chillie powder, turmeric powder and salt with 4 tablespoons of olive oil to make a paste. Thoroughly blend the spices with the chicken and allow to marinate for 2 hours in the refrigerator.
2. Sauté onions in a pan with 4 tablespoons of olive oil till onion is lightly browned.
3. Add marinated chicken cubes and stir. Cover and cook, stirring occasionally, on medium heat for approximately 20 minutes.
4. Add diced potatoes and allow to cook for 10 to 15 minutes, stirring occasionally or until chicken and potatoes are thoroughly cooked. Set aside to cool.

**Continued on next page**

# Samosas cont.

## Samosa Pastry

### Ingredients:

4 cups all purpose wheat flour
1 teaspoon salt
4 tablespoons olive oil
2 - 3 cups cold water
½ cup extra flour for rolling out
½ cup extra olive oil to spread on pastries

### Method:

1. Mix salt and 4 tablespoons olive oil in the flour and bind with cold water. Knead to make a soft dough.
2. Take 1½ inch round balls of dough and roll out with a velan or rolling pin. Make 20 to 25 two inch flat rounds.  Spread oil completely over the surface area of the 2 inch round pastries.  Sprinkle each lightly with flour.
3. Join two, 2 inch round flats together with the oiled sides facing each other. Press the two together gently with your hand. This is now ready to roll again. Flour both sides of the double 2 inch flats and roll out to about a 6 to 8 inch round roti.
4. Heat a tawa or flat frying pan on medium heat.  Place roti on hot pan and cook lightly on one side then turn the roti over and cook lightly on the other side, for approximately 20 seconds.
5. Remove roti and place on a clean tea towel.  Separate the two rotis from each other at the point where they were joined before rolling.  The rotis will separate easily.
6. Place rotis covered in the tea towel so that the rotis do not dry out.
7. *Once the rotis are all made and piled on top of each other, cut them into 3 inch wide strips with the edges at an angle.  This gives the pastry a trapezoid shape.

* Keep the ends and deep fry them until crispy golden brown.  Sprinkle with salt and serve or sprinkle with sugar and cinnamon powder and serve.  Makes a great snack.

**Continued on next page**

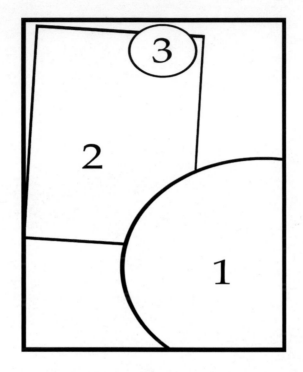

Pakoras see page 19

# Samosas cont.

## Paste

### Ingredients:

6 tablespoons all purpose flour
1 to 2 cups warm water

### Method:

Stir in enough water to make a runny paste, the consistency of a pan-cake dough.  Mix the paste thoroughly till paste is free of lumps.

## Folding, Filling, Storing and Cooking Methods

1. Brush paste on side A and fold onto side B (see figure 1).
2. Apply paste on the top side of side A, then fold side C onto the glued area, making sure side C folds over leaving a flap (see figure 2).
3. Fill the samosa in the opening of the triangular pocket.  Approximately 1 to 1½ tablespoons filling will be needed to fill the samosa. Brush paste on the flap and close samosa, to make a triangular shaped samosa.
4. At this point samosas can be stored in a freezer bag and frozen for later use.
5. Deep fry samosas on medium heat for 5 to 7 minutes or till samosas are golden brown.  Or bake samosas on a non-greased cookie sheet in a preheated oven at 375°F, for 7 minutes on each side.

Samosas make great appetizers served with cilantro chutney (page 77) or tamarind chutney (page 78).

# Samosas cont.

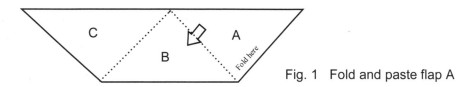

Fig. 1   Fold and paste flap A

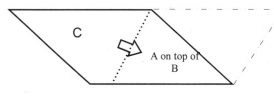

Fig. 2   Fold and paste flap C

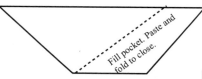

Fig. 3   Fill pocket with filling and paste

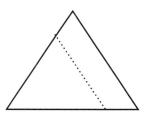

Fig. 4  Completed Samosa

# Pakoras

## Ingredients:

1 cup chana flour
2 tablespoons all purpose flour
2 teaspoons ginger/garlic masala
1 teaspoon green chillie masala
1 teaspoon turmeric powder
1 teaspoon baking powder
1 teaspoon red chillie powder
2 teaspoons garam masala
2 teaspoons salt
4 tablespoons olive oil
1 to 2 cups water

1 cup finely chopped spinach
1 small potato grated
1 medium onion finely chopped
½ cup grated zucchini
4 cups of oil for frying

## Method:

1. Mix chana flour, all purpose flour, baking powder, 4 tablespoons of olive oil, ginger/garlic masala, green chillie masala, red chillie powder, turmeric powder , garam masala and salt in large bowl.  Add water and stir till mixture is the consistency of a cake mix.
2. Add grated potato, chopped onion, grated zucchini and chopped spinach to the dough and stir.
3. Heat oil in a wok or deep fryer on medium heat.  Carefully drop about a tablespoon of the mixture, into the heated oil.
4. Allow the pakora to cook for about 2 to 3 minutes, turning occasionally.  Remove pakora when they are crispy golden brown.

Serve pakora with tamarind chutney (see page 78)

# Spicy Chicken Wings

## Ingredients:

3 lbs chicken wings
4 teaspoons ginger/garlic masala
1 teaspoon green chillie masala
2 teaspoons garam masala
2 teaspoons  thana jeeroo
1 teaspoon red chillie powder
2 teaspoons paprika
1 teaspoon turmeric powder
2 teaspoons salt
8 tablespoons olive oil
4 tablespoons chopped cilantro

## Method:

1. Mix ginger/garlic masala, green chillie masala, red chillie powder, turmeric powder, garam masala, thana jeeroo, paprika and salt with 3 tablespoons of olive oil to make a spice paste.
2. Thoroughly blend in the spice paste with the wings and marinate for at least 2 hours in the refrigerator.
3. Heat 5 tablespoons of olive oil in frying pan or wok on medium heat.  Add wings and stir.  Cover and cook for 20 to 30 minutes turning the wings occasionally or till wings are thoroughly cooked and golden brown.
4. Serve hot and garnish with chopped cilantro.

Serve with cilantro chutney (page 77) or spicy tomato sauce (page 81).

# Eggplant Papeta

## Ingredients:

1 large eggplant sliced
1½ teaspoons ginger/garlic masala
½ teaspoon green chillie masala
1 teaspoon thana jeeroo
½ teaspoon red chillie powder
½ teaspoon turmeric powder
1 teaspoon salt
8 tablespoons olive oil
¼ cup all purpose flour

## Method:

1. In a bowl mix ginger/garlic masala, green chillie masala, thana jeeroo, red chillie powder, turmeric powder and salt with 2 tablespoons of olive oil to make a spice paste.
2. Slice eggplant into about ¼ inch thick slices. Spread spice paste on both sides of the eggplant slices.
3. Dip eggplant in flour, covering both sides.
4. Shallow fry in a frying pan with 6 tablespoons of olive oil on medium heat.  Cook 3 to 5 minutes on each side or till eggplant is well cooked.

Serve with hot roti (page 63) or naan (page 64).   Makes great sandwiches.

# Spicy Chicken Pita

## Spicy Chicken Mixture

### Ingredients:

4 chicken breasts cubed
1 teaspoon garam masala
1 teaspoon thana jeeroo
1½ teaspoons salt
1 teaspoon turmeric
½ teaspoon red chillie powder
1 teaspoon ginger/garlic masala
1 teaspoon green chillie masala
6 tablespoons olive oil

### Method:

1. Wash and drain cubed chicken breasts.
2. Mix ginger/garlic masala, green chillie masala, garam masala, thana jeeroo, red chillie powder, turmeric and salt with 2 tablespoons of olive oil to make spice paste.
3. Marinate chicken with the spice paste for 2 hours in the refrigerator.
4. Heat 4 tablespoons of olive oil in a frying pan. Add marinated chicken pieces and stir.
5. Stir occasionally and cook for 20 minutes on medium heat or till chicken is thoroughly cooked.

**Continued on next page**

# Spicy Chicken Pita cont.

## Putting Naan (Pita) Together

### Ingredients:

spicy chicken mixture (see page 22)
1 tomato diced
1 small onion chopped finely
½ cup spicy tomato sauce (see page 81)
½ head iceberg lettuce chopped finely
6 naans cut in half (see page 64)
1 cup grated cheese
mustard (optional)

### Method:

1. Open one half of the naan and put in a handful of spicy chicken mixture.
2. Spread about a tablespoon of spicy tomato sauce and squeeze some mustard inside pita. Sprinkle with chopped onions, tomatoes, grated cheese and lettuce.

Great for lunches or appetizers.

# Vagarela Rice (Fried Rice)

## Ingredients:

2 cups cooked rice
1 onion finely chopped
1 large potato diced
½ cup chopped celery
1 teaspoon ginger/garlic masala
½ teaspoon green chillie masala
½ teaspoon turmeric powder
½ teaspoon red chillie powder
1 teaspoon salt
1 teaspoon cumin seeds
1 teaspoon black mustard seeds
1 tablespoon sesame seeds
1 tablespoon chopped cilantro
4 tablespoons olive oil
¼ cup water

## Method:

1. In a pan heat olive oil. Add cumin seeds and black mustard seeds and allow to pop.
2. Add chopped onions. Sauté till lightly browned.
3. Add potato, celery, ginger/garlic masala, green chillie masala, turmeric powder, red chillie powder and salt. Allow to cook covered on medium heat for 10 to 15 minutes, stirring occasionally.
4. Add cooked rice and stir.
5. Add water and allow to cook on low heat for 10 to 15 minutes.
6. Garnish with sesame seeds and chopped cilantro.

One of our favorite family lunches, made with left-over rice.

# Meat, Poultry & Fish Dishes

# Meat, Poultry & Fish Dishes

# Butter Chicken

## Ingredients:

1½ lbs chicken pieces
2 teaspoons ginger/garlic masala
1 teaspoon green chillie masala
1 teaspoon garam masala
1 teaspoon thana jeeroo
1 teaspoon red chillie powder
1 teaspoon turmeric powder
2 teaspoons salt
½ medium onion finely chopped
3 tablespoons olive oil
6 tablespoons ghee or butter

¾ cup half and half cream
¾ cup yogurt
¼ cup tomato sauce
1 cup water (optional)
2 tablespoons chopped cilantro

## Method:

1. Mix together, ginger/garlic masala, green chillie masala, garam masala, thana jeeroo, red chillie powder, turmeric powder and salt with 1 tablespoon of olive oil to make a spice paste.
2. Wash and drain chicken, then marinate with the spice paste for at least 2 hours in the refrigerator.
3. Heat ghee in a pan. Add chopped onions. Sauté till lightly browned.
4. Add marinated chicken to the onions and stir. Cover and allow to cook on medium heat for 20 to 30 minutes or till chicken is thoroughly cooked.
5. Add cream and cook on medium heat for 5 to 10 minutes.
6. Add yogurt and water (optional - for a thicker sauce reduce the amount of water or do not add water). Stir.
7. Add tomato sauce and allow to cook for another 5 to 10 minutes on low heat. Garnish with chopped cilantro.

Serve on a bed of basmati rice (page 67) or with hot roti (page 63), naan (page 64) or foolecha (page 66).

# Spicy Baked Pepper Chicken

## Ingredients:

3 lbs chicken breast
2 teaspoons garam masala
2 teaspoons thana jeeroo
½ teaspoon red chillie powder
1 teaspoon turmeric powder
1 teaspoon paprika
1 teaspoon black pepper crushed
2 teaspoons oregano
2 teaspoons sweet basil
2 teaspoons salt
4 tablespoons olive oil

3 potatoes
2 carrots
1 cup broccoli
1 green pepper
1 red pepper
1 onion cut in four
3 garlic cloves

## Method:

1. Mix together olive oil, garam masala, thana jeeroo, red chillie powder, turmeric powder and salt to make a spice paste.
2. Marinade the chicken with the spice paste and place in refrigerator for 2 hours.
3. Cut potatoes, broccoli and onion in large chunks. Julienne carrots, green pepper and red pepper.
4. Place marinated chicken in a roasting pan. Cover chicken with potatoes, onions, carrots, broccoli, green pepper and red pepper.
5. Sprinkle with oregano, sweet basil, pepper and paprika.
6. Slice garlic into thin slivers and sprinkle over the vegetables.
7. Cover and bake in a preheated oven at 375°F for 60 to 80 minutes or till chicken and vegetables are thoroughly cooked.

# Chicken Curry

## Ingredients:

3 lbs chicken pieces
4 teaspoons ginger/garlic masala
1 teaspoon green chillie masala
3 teaspoons garam masala
2 teaspoons thana jeeroo
1 teaspoon red chillie powder
1 teaspoon turmeric powder
2 teaspoons salt
3 medium onions chopped
1 medium tomato diced
1½ cups tomato sauce
8 tablespoons olive oil
2 cassia sticks (also known as cinnamon bark)

2 cardamoms
2 cloves
4 black peppercorns
2 tablespoons chopped cilantro
1 cup water

## Method:

1. Mix ginger/garlic masala, green chillie masala, garam masala, thana jeeroo, red chillie powder, turmeric powder and salt with 4 table-spoons of olive oil, to make a paste.
2. Thoroughly blend the spices with the chicken and allow to marinate for 2 hours in the refrigerator.
3. Heat 4 tablespoons of olive oil in a pan and add cassia sticks, carda-moms, cloves and peppercorns to flavor the oil. Add chopped on-ions. Sauté.
4. Add marinated chicken and stir. Cover and cook on medium heat for approximately 20 minutes, stirring occasionally.
5. Add tomato sauce, water and diced tomatoes to the curry.
6. Cook covered on medium heat for 20 - 30 minutes until curry is nice and thick and chicken is thoroughly cooked. Garnish with chopped cilantro.

Serve hot over a bed of basmati rice (p 67) or with hot roti (p 63), naan (p 64) or foolecha (p 66).

# Ba's Biryani

## Chicken Tapeli

### Ingredients:

3 lbs chicken, cleaned and cubed
4 teaspoons ginger/garlic masala
1 teaspoon green chillie masala
3 teaspoons garam masala
3 teaspoons thana jeeroo
1 teaspoon red chillie powder
1 teaspoon turmeric powder
2 teaspoons salt
1 medium onion chopped
8 tablespoons olive oil

### Method:

1. Mix ginger/garlic masala, green chillie masala, garam masala, thana jeeroo, red chillie powder, turmeric powder and salt with 3 tablespoons of olive oil, to make a paste.
2. Thoroughly blend the spices with the chicken and allow to marinate for 2 hours in the refrigerator.
3. Heat 5 tablespoons of olive oil in a pan and add chopped onion. Sauté till lightly browned.
4. Add marinated chicken and stir. Cover and cook, stirring occasionally on medium heat for approximately 30 - 40 minutes or till chicken is thoroughly cooked.

Every time I make this dish it brings back fond memories of my childhood, when my mother cooked her Biryani for us. Those were special days.

**Continued on next page**

# Ba's Biryani cont.

## Basmati Rice with Whole Cumin and Onions

## Ingredients:

3 cups basmati rice
½ onion finely sliced
2 teaspoons cumin seeds
2 tablespoons ghee
3 cups water
3 teaspoons salt

## Method:

1. Wash rice in warm water under the tap, rinsing the rice 3 times.
2. Heat ghee in a pot and allow to melt. Add cumin seeds and sliced onion. Sauté.
3. Add washed rice, water and salt. Stir and cook covered on medium heat.
4. Allow to cook for 20 - 30 minutes or until rice is thoroughly cooked.
5. Check rice occasionally to make sure it is not sticking. To avoid sticking add water only if rice is not cooked and there is no water visible in the pot.

**Continued on next page**

# Ba's Biryani cont.

## Putting the Biryani Together

### Ingredients:

chicken tapeli (see page 30)
cooked basmati rice with cumin and onions (see page 31)
2 teaspoons saffron (optional)
6 tablespoons chopped cilantro
2 tablespoons ghee
750 ml yogurt

### Method:

1. Grease the bottom of a large deep pot or pressure cooker with ghee.
2. Spread a 1 inch layer of cooked rice mixture on the bottom of the pot.
3. Spread about ¼ cup yogurt on top of the layer of rice and sprinkle with a small amount of saffron.
4. Add a layer of chicken tapeli, about an inch thick.
5. Add another layer of cooked rice mixture on the curry and continue steps 2 to 4 until you come to the top of pot. Leave a space of 1 inch on top, before covering with the lid. Make sure the lid sits tight on the pot. Make sure that the top layer is rice with yogurt. Sprinkle with saffron.
6. Allow to cook covered on low heat for approximately 30 to 40 minutes.

When serving, cut through the layers of the Biryani and place on a flat serving dish. Garnish with cilantro.

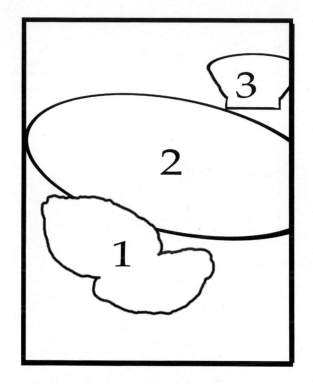

1. Foolecha see page 66
2. Chicken Curry see page 29
3. Cilantro Chutney see page 77

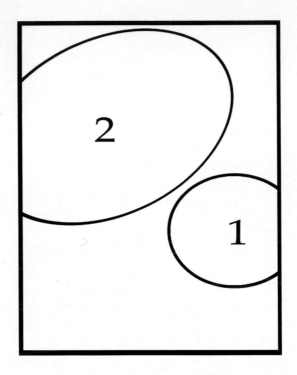

# Stuffed Green Peppers & Potatoes

## Ingredients:

2 lbs ground beef
3 teaspoons ginger/garlic masala
1 teaspoon green chillie masala
2 teaspoons garam masala
2 teaspoons thana jeeroo
½ teaspoon red chillie powder
1 teaspoon turmeric powder
1½ teaspoons salt
1 medium onion grated

2 green bell peppers
4 medium potatoes
7 tablespoons olive oil
2 cassia sticks
1 cardamom
2 cloves
4 peppercorns

## Method:

1. Mix together ginger/garlic masala, green chillie masala, garam masala, thana jeeroo, red chillie powder, turmeric powder and salt with 3 tablespoons of olive oil.
2. Thoroughly blend the paste with the ground beef. Allow the meat to marinate for 2 hours in the refrigerator.
3. Grate onion and squeeze to remove any excess water. Blend the grated onion with the marinated ground beef
4. Peel and core the potatoes In the center using an apple oorer Wash and cut green peppers in half and remove all the seeds.
5. Fill the cored potatoes and green peppers with the marinated beef.
6. With any remaining beef, make 1 to 2 inch sized meat balls and set aside.
7. Heat 4 tablespoons of olive oil in a saucepan and add cassia sticks, cardamom, cloves and peppercorns to flavor the oil.
8. Place stuffed potatoes and peppers, meat side facing down, in the pan. Add meat balls and cover. Allow to cook on low heat for 20 minutes.
9. Stir occasionally, taking care not to break the potatoes or peppers so the filling stays intact. Allow to cook for another 20 minutes or until meat and vegetables are thoroughly cooked.

# Spicy Beef Stir fry

## Ingredients:

2 sirloin steaks
3 potatoes
1 green pepper
1 chopped onion
2 teaspoons garam masala
2 teaspoons thana jeeroo
1 teaspoon turmeric powder
1 teaspoon red chillie powder
1 teaspoon crushed black pepper
2 teaspoons salt
3 garlic cloves sliced
1 ginger cube sliced
4 tablespoons olive oil

## Method:

1. Slice steak into 2 inch by ¼ inch strips. Wash and allow to drain.
2. Make a paste with 1 tablespoon olive oil, garam masala, thana jeeroo, turmeric powder, red chillie   powder, pepper and salt.
3. Marinate the beef with the paste until evenly spread. Allow to marinate in refrigerator for 2 hours.
4. In a pan heat 3 tablespoons olive oil. Add sliced garlic and ginger. Sauté.   Add chopped onion and sauté.
5. Add beef strips and stir. Allow beef to cook on medium heat for about 10 to 15 minutes and cook     covered.
6. Add chopped potatoes and allow to cook for another 10 minutes.
7. Add sliced green peppers and allow to cook for another 10 to 15 minutes or till meat and vegetables are cooked.

# Spicy Lamb with Cabbage

## Ingredients:

3 lbs lamb cubed
1 medium onion chopped
1 medium sized cabbage chopped finely
2 teaspoons ginger/garlic masala
1 teaspoon green chillie masala
2 teaspoons garam masala
2 teaspoons thana jeeroo
1 teaspoon turmeric powder
½ teaspoon red chillie powder
2 teaspoons salt
2 tablespoons chopped cilantro

7 tablespoons olive oil
2 cassia sticks
1 cardamom
2 cloves
4 peppercorns

## Method:

1. Mix ginger/garlic masala, green chillie masala, garam masala, thana jeeroo, red chillie powder, turmeric powder and salt with 3 tablespoons of olive oil to make a paste.
2. Thoroughly blend the spices with the lamb and allow to marinate for 2 hours in the refrigerator.
3. Heat 4 tablespoons of olive oil in a pot and add cassia sticks, cardamom, cloves and peppercorns to flavor the oil. Add chopped onion. Sauté.
4. Add marinated lamb and stir. Cover and cook on medium heat for 20 minutes stirring occasionally.
5. Add chopped cabbage over the lamb and allow to cook on low heat for another 10 to 15 minutes or till both lamb and cabbage are thoroughly cooked.
6. Garnish with chopped cilantro.

Serve hot with roti (page 63) or naan (page 64) bread.

# Shrimp Curry

## Ingredients:

1 lb shrimp
1 teaspoon garlic masala
½ teaspoon green chillie masala
2 teaspoons crushed cumin
1 teaspoon thana jeeroo
½ teaspoon red chillie powder
½ teaspoon turmeric powder
1 teaspoon salt
1 cup chopped green onions
1 medium tomato diced
1 cup tomato sauce
4 tablespoons olive oil

## Method:

1. Heat saucepan and add tomato sauce, ½ teaspoon garlic masala, ½ teaspoon thana jeeroo, 1 teaspoon crushed cumin, ¼ teaspoon red chillie powder, ¼ teaspoon turmeric powder and ½ teaspoon salt. Stir.
2. Heat till sauce comes to a boil and set aside.
3. In a pan heat olive oil. Add green onions and sauté.
4. Add the rest of the garlic masala, green chillie masala, thana jeeroo, crushed cumin, red chillie powder, turmeric powder and salt. Stir.
5. Add shrimp to the sauce and allow to cook for 5 to 10 minutes.
6. Add diced tomatoes to the shrimp sauce mixture. Cook for another 10 to 15 minutes or till shrimp and tomatoes are cooked.

Serve over a hot bed of basmati rice (page 67).

# Boiled Egg Curry

## Ingredients:

6 boiled eggs
1 onion chopped
½ cup chopped green onions
1 tomato diced
1 teaspoon ginger/garlic masala
¼ teaspoon green chillie masala
1½ teaspoons garam masala
½ teaspoon thana jeeroo
½ teaspoon red chillie powder
½ teaspoon turmeric powder
3 tablespoons olive oil
1 teaspoon salt
1 cup tomato sauce
2 tablespoons chopped cilantro

## Method:

1. Peel and cut boiled eggs in half and set aside.
2. In a pot heat olive oil and add chopped onion and green onions. Sauté while stirring.
3. Add ginger/garlic masala, green chillie masala, ½ teaspoon garam masala, thana jeeroo, red chillie powder, turmeric powder and salt. Stir.
4. Add diced tomato and tomato sauce. Stir. Cover and allow to cook for 10 to 15 minutes on medium heat, stirring occassionally.
5. Place the halved boiled eggs gently in the sauce, cover and allow to cook on low heat for 10 minutes.
6. Garnish with chopped cilantro and sprinkle with 1 teaspoon garam masala.

One of my Mom's favorite quick dishes for those, "I don't know what to cook" days.

# Scrambled Egg Curry

## Ingredients:

4 eggs
1 small onion chopped
½ cup chopped green onions
½ teaspoon ginger/garlic masala
¼ teaspoon green chillie masala
¼ teaspoon garam masala
¼ teaspoon thana jeeroo
¼ teaspoon red chillie powder
¼ teaspoon turmeric powder
½ teaspoon salt
¼ teaspoon pepper
¼ cup milk
4 tablespoons ghee or olive oil

## Method:

1. Crack eggs in a bowl. Add ginger/garlic masala, green chillie masala, garam masala, thana jeeroo, red chillie powder, turmeric powder, milk, salt and pepper.
2. Whisk the mixture thoroughly for 2 minutes.
3. In a frying pan heat ghee or olive oil and add chopped onion and chopped green onions. Sauté.
4. Add mixture and stir constantly until egg is cooked.

Serve scrambled eggs with hot roti (page 63) or toast. Great breakfast meal!

# Spicy Meat Ball Curry

## Ingredients:

3 lbs ground beef
4 teaspoons ginger/garlic masala
1 teaspoon green chillie masala
3 teaspoons garam masala
2 teaspoons thana jeeroo
1 teaspoon red chillie powder
1 teaspoon turmeric powder
2 teaspoons salt
2 medium onions chopped
8 tablespoons olive oil

1½ cups tomato sauce
2 medium tomatoes diced
2 cassia sticks
2 cardamom
2 cloves
4 peppercorns
1 tablespoon vinegar
1½ cups warm water
4 tablespoons chopped cilantro

## Method:

1. Mix ginger/garlic masala, green chillie masala, garam masala, thana jeeroo, red chillie powder, turmeric powder and salt with 4 tablespoons of olive oil to make a paste. Thoroughly blend the paste with ground beef.
2. Allow meat to marinate for at least 2 hours in the fridge.
3. Grate onions and squeeze to remove excess water. Mix grated onion and 4 tablespoons of chopped cilantro with ground beef.
4. Heat 4 tablespoons of olive oil in a pan. Add cassia sticks, cardamoms, cloves and peppercorns to the hot oil.
5. In a separate bowl, mix vinegar with ½ cup of warm water. Use to dampen fingers before shaping the meat balls.
6. Make meat balls into 1 to 2 inch rounds. Place meatballs in heated pan with whole spices on medium heat.
7. Cover and allow to cook for 5 minutes before stirring. Continue to cook for 20 minutes stirring occasionally.
8. Add tomato sauce, 1 cup of warm water and diced tomatoes to the meat balls.
9. Cover on medium heat for 20 to 30 minutes until curry is thick and meat balls are thoroughly cooked. Garnish with chopped cilantro.

# Notes

# Spicy
# Vegetable
# Dishes

# *Spicy Vegetable Dishes*

# Cauliflower Potato Curry

## Ingredients:

1 small cauliflower
1 onion chopped
2 tomatoes diced
2 potatoes diced
2 cups frozen peas
2 teaspoons ginger/garlic masala
½ teaspoon green chillie masala
2 teaspoons thana jeeroo
1 teaspoon red chillie powder
1 teaspoon turmeric powder
1 teaspoon cumin seeds
1 teaspoon black mustard seeds
2 teaspoons salt
4 tablespoons olive oil
2 tablespoons chopped cilantro

## Method:

1. Heat olive oil in a pan and add cumin seeds, black mustard seeds and chopped onion. Sauté.
2. Cut cauliflower into small pieces. Add cauliflower and diced potatoes to the onions and stir.
3. Add ginger/garlic masala, green chillie masala, thana jeeroo, red chillie powder, turmeric powder and salt. Stir.
4. Cover and allow to cook on medium heat for 10 minutes, stirring occasionally.
5. Add frozen peas and allow to cook for another 5 to 10 minutes.
6. Add diced tomatoes and cook for another 10 minutes on low heat or till vegetables are thoroughly cooked.
7. Garnish with chopped cilantro.

# Spinach Curry

## Ingredients:

8 cups chopped spinach
1 onion chopped
2 tomatoes diced
2 teaspoons ginger/garlic masala
¼ teaspoon green chillie masala
1 teaspoon thana jeeroo
1 teaspoon turmeric powder
1 teaspoon red chillie powder
3 teaspoons cumin seeds
4 tablespoons olive oil
2 potatoes diced
1½ teaspoons salt

## Method:

1. Heat olive oil in a pan on medium heat and add cumin seeds and chopped onion.  Sauté.
2. Add and stir in ginger/garlic masala, green chillie masala, thana jeeroo, turmeric powder, red chillie powder and salt.
3. Add diced potatoes and stir.  Cook covered for 5 minutes.
4. Add  chopped spinach.  Cover and allow to cook for 15 minutes, stirring occasionally.
5. Add diced tomatoes and allow to cook for another 10 minutes on low heat.

# Eggplant Potato Curry

## Ingredients:

1 large eggplant
1 potato diced
1 onion chopped finely
2 tomatoes diced
1 teaspoon ginger/garlic masala
½ teaspoon green chillie masala
1 teaspoon thana jeeroo
½ teaspoon red chillie powder
1 teaspoon turmeric powder
1 teaspoon cumin seeds
1 teaspoon salt
4 tablespoons olive oil

## Method:

1. Sauté cumin seeds and chopped onion in a pan with olive oil.
2. Cut eggplant into small one inch cubes. Peel and dice potato to ½ inch cubes.
3. Add potato and eggplant to the pan and stir.
4. Add ginger/garlic masala, green chillie masala, thana jeeroo, red chillie powder, turmeric powder and salt. Stir. Allow to cook covered on low heat for 15 to 20 minutes stirring occasionaly.
5. Add diced tomatoes and allow to cook for another 10 minutes or till all the vegetables are cooked.

# Okra Curry

## Ingredients:

2 cups sliced okra
1 chopped onion
2 tomatoes diced
1 teaspoon ginger/garlic masala
½ teaspoon green chillie masala
1 teaspoon thana jeeroo
1 teaspoon cumin seeds
½ teaspoon turmeric powder
½ teaspoon red chillie powder
1½ teaspoons salt
6 tablespoons olive oil

## Method:

1. Heat olive oil in a pan, on medium heat.  Add cumin seeds and chopped onion.  Sauté.
2. Add sliced okra, ginger/garlic masala, green chillie masala, thana jeeroo, turmeric powder, red chillie powder and salt.  Stir.
3. Cover and continue cooking on low heat for 10 to 15 minutes, stirring occasionally.
4. Add diced tomatoes and cook covered for another 10 minutes until both the okra and tomatoes are cooked.

# Raveya (Stuffed Eggplant)

## Ingredients:

6 to 8 small eggplants
1 small onion chopped
3 tablespoons crushed unsalted peanuts
1½ teaspoons ginger/garlic masala
½ teaspoon green chillie masala
1 teaspoon thana jeeroo
½ teaspoon red chillie powder
½ teaspoon turmeric powder
1 teaspoon salt
4 tablespoons olive oil
1 tablespoon chopped cilantro

## Method:

1. Mix chopped onion, crushed peanuts, ginger/garlic masala, green chillie masala, thana jeeroo, red chillie powder, turmeric powder, salt and chopped cilantro to make a crumbly stuffing.
2. Wash and cut eggplant in quarters making sure not to cut right through the bottom. Leave ¾ inch of the eggplant uncut so that the eggplant still holds together.
3. Stuff each of the eggplants evenly with the stuffing, using up all of the stuffing.
4. In a pan heat olive oil on low heat and gently place the stuffed eggplants in the pan, standing upright.
5. Cover and allow to cook for 15 to 20 minutes or till eggplants are thoroughly cooked.

# Spicy Pepper & Potato Dish

## Ingredients:

½ a green bell pepper
2 large potatoes
1 medium tomato
1 medium onion
1 teaspoon ginger/garlic masala
¼ teaspoon green chillie masala
½ teaspoon red chillie powder
½ teaspoon turmeric powder
1 teaspoon thana jeeroo
1½ teaspoons salt
1 teaspoon cumin seeds
4 tablespoons olive oil

## Method:

1. Peel and cut potatoes into 1 inch cubes.  Slice green pepper and onion and set aside.
2. In a frying pan heat olive oil on medium heat.  Add cumin seeds and allow the seeds to pop.
3. As soon as the seeds pop, add the potatoes, green peppers and onion.  Stir.
4. Add ginger/garlic masala, green chillie masala, thana jeeroo, red chillie powder, turmeric powder and salt.  Stir till all the spices are evenly mixed.
5. Cover and cook for 10 minutes on medium heat, stirring occasionally.
6. Add diced tomatoes and cook for another 10 minutes on low heat till all the vegetables are thoroughly cooked.

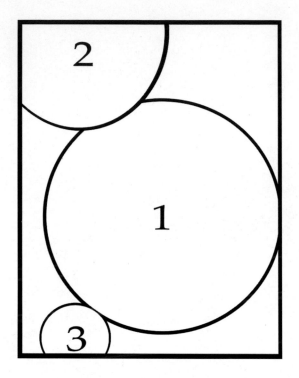

1. Cauliflower Potato Curry see page 43
2. Yellow Rice with Onions see page 68
3. Raita see page 74

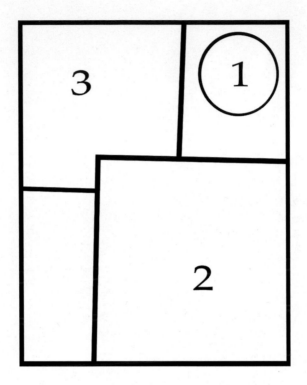

1. Apple Pickle see page 73
2. Spicy Beef Stir Fry see page 34
3. Spicy Corn see page 49

# Spicy Corn with Red Peppers

## Ingredients:

4 cups corn kernels
1 red pepper diced
1 teaspoon ginger/garlic masala
¼ teaspoon green chillie masala
½ teaspoon red chillie powder
½ teaspoon turmeric powder
1 teaspoon salt
½ teaspoon black mustard seeds
2 teaspoons sesame seeds
4 tablespoons olive oil
2 tablespoons chopped cilantro
juice of ½ lemon

## Method:

1. In a bowl add corn, ginger/garlic masala, green chillie masala, red chillie powder, turmeric powder and salt.
2. Heat olive oil in a pan. Add black mustard seeds and allow the seeds to pop.
3. Add the corn, spices and lemon juice to the pan and stir.
4. Cover and allow to cook on medium heat for 10 minutes.
5. Add diced red pepper and cook for another 5 minutes.
6. Garnish with chopped cilantro and sesame seeds.

# Ginger/Garlic Potatoes

## Ingredients:

2 medium potatoes diced
1 teaspoon ginger/garlic masala
½ teaspoon green chillie masala
1 teaspoon turmeric powder
1 teaspoon cumin seeds
1 teaspoon salt
2 teaspoons sesame seeds
1 tablespoon chopped cilantro
3 tablespoons ghee

## Method:

1. Peel and cut potatoes into ½ inch cubes.
2. Heat ghee on medium heat in a frying pan and add cumin seeds.
3. Add potatoes, ginger/garlic masala, green chillie masala, turmeric powder, and salt. Stir.
4. Cover and allow to cook on low heat for 15 to 20 minutes stirring occasionally or till potatoes are thoroughly cooked.
5. Garnish with chopped cilantro and sesame seeds.

# Spicy Baked Potatoes

## Ingredients:

4 large potatoes
½ teaspoon ginger/garlic masala
¼ teaspoon green chillie masala
1 teaspoon crushed cumin
½ teaspoon turmeric powder
1 teaspoon salt
4 tablespoons butter
1 tablespoon chopped cilantro

## Method:

1. Wash potatoes thoroughly.  Core the center of the potato with an apple corer.
2. Mix together ginger/garlic masala, green chillie masala, crushed cumin, turmeric powder, chopped cilantro and salt with butter.
3. Take small amounts of the spiced butter and fill the cored potatoes.
4. Plug the ends of the potato with small pieces of the cored potato.
5. Wrap potato in thick tin foil and cook on the barbecue on medium heat.
6. Turn potatoes occasionally and allow to cook for 30 minutes or till potatoes are thoroughly cooked.

# Vegetable Pilaf

## Ingredients:

2 medium potatoes diced
2 carrots chopped
1 small yam diced
1 small sweet potato diced
2 cups frozen peas
1 medium onion chopped
2 teaspoons ginger/garlic masala
1 teaspoon green chillie masala
2 teaspoons thana jeeroo
1 teaspoon red chillie powder
1 teaspoon turmeric powder
1 teaspoon cumin seeds
1½ teaspoons salt

1 tablespoon sesame seeds
½ cup water
4 tablespoons olive oil
1 tablespoon chopped cilantro
2 cups basmati rice
2 teaspoons salt
2 cups water

## Method:

1. Wash basmati rice 3 times and cook in a pan with 2 cups of water and 2 teaspoons salt.
2. Allow the rice to cook on medium heat for about 10 to 15 minutes or till rice is half cooked. Remove from the stove and drain off water in a sieve and set aside.
3. Heat olive oil in a large pot and add cumin seeds and chopped onion. Sauté. Add diced potatoes, carrots, yam, sweet potatoes and peas. Stir in ginger/garlic masala, green chillie masala, thana jeeroo, red chillie powder, turmeric powder and salt.
4. Cover and allow to cook on medium heat for 10 minutes, stirring the vegetables occasionally.
5. Spread the half cooked basmati rice over top of the vegetables and add ½ cup of water. Cover and cook pilaf on low heat for 15 to 20 minutes or till rice and vegetables are thoroughly cooked.
6. Serve on a large platter and garnish with sesame seeds and chopped cilantro.

# *Spicy Lentil Dishes*

# *Spicy
Lentil Dishes*

# Chevtee Daal

## Ingredients:

1 cup toower daal
1 cup urad daal
1½ teaspoons ginger/garlic masala
½ teaspoon green chillie masala
¼ teaspoon red chillie powder
½ teaspoon turmeric powder
1 teaspoon salt
4 tablespoons ghee
2 teaspoons garam masala
3 cups water

## Method:

1. Wash and rinse both the daals.
2. Cook in a pressure cooker with 3 cups of water, until daals are cooked to a pulp.
3. Strain daal through a fine sieve in a dish.
4. Add red chillie powder, turmeric powder, 1 teaspoon garam masala and salt to the sieved daal and stir.
5. In a pot melt ghee on medium heat.  Add ginger/garlic masala and green chillie masala.  Sauté.
6. Add the daal to the ghee and stir.  Cover and allow the daal to come to a boil, stirring constantly.
7. Sprinkle 1 teaspoon of garam masala over the cooked daal to garnish.

# Mung Daal Curry

## Ingredients:

1 cup mung daal
1 teaspoon ginger/garlic masala
½ teaspoon green chillie masala
¼ teaspoon red chillie powder
½ teaspoon turmeric powder
½ teaspoon salt
3 tablespoons olive oil

## Method:

1. Wash and soak mung daal in warm water for approximately 2 hours or till daal expands to twice its size.
2. Wash daal again and drain off any excess water.
3. Add, ginger/garlic masala, green chillie masala, red chillie powder, turmeric powder and salt to the daal.
4. Heat olive oil in a pan on medium heat. Add the spiced daal mixture and stir.
5. Pour just enough water in the pan to cover the daal. Allow to cook on low heat for 20 to 30 minutes or till daal is thoroughly cooked.

# Chana Daal with Zucchini

## Ingredients:

1 cup chana daal
1 small zucchini
1 teaspoon ginger/garlic masala
¼ teaspoon green chillie masala
½ teaspoon red chillie powder
½ teaspoon turmeric powder
½ teaspoon black mustard seeds
½ teaspoon salt
3 tablespoons olive oil
½ cup water
3 tablespoons chopped cilantro

## Method:

1. Soak chana daal in warm water for about 3 hours until daal expands to twice its original size.
2. Wash chana daal and drain off excess water. Add ginger/garlic masala, green chillie masala, red chillie powder, turmeric powder and salt to the daal.
3. Heat olive oil in a pan on medium heat. Add black mustard seeds and allow the seeds to pop in the hot oil.
4. Add chana daal to the spices in the pan and stir. Add ½ cup of water and allow to cook covered on medium heat for 10 to 15 minutes or till daal is half cooked.
5. Add chopped zucchini over the daal. Cover and allow to cook on low heat for another 10 minutes or till both the daal and the zucchini is cooked.
6. Garnish with chopped cilantro.

# Vadhu (Sprouted Bean Curry)

**Ingredients:**

1 cup mung beans
1½ teaspoons ginger/garlic masala
½ teaspoon green chillie masala
¼ teaspoon red chillie powder
¼ teaspoon turmeric powder
¾ teaspoon salt
1 medium onion chopped
4 tablespoons olive oil
¼ cup water

## Method:

1. Soak mung beans in warm water for approximately 3 hours or till mung beans increase to twice their original size.
2. Drain and tie mung beans in a clean cheese cloth, and place in a deep dish. Place the beans in a dark place for approximately 24 hours.
3. After 24 hours open the cloth and you will find the beans have sprouted.
4. Remove sprouted beans from the cloth. Wash the beans thoroughly and drain in a colander.
5. Place sprouted mung beans in a large saucepan and add olive oil, finely chopped onion, ginger/garlic masala, green chillie masala, red chillie powder, turmeric powder, water and salt. Stir.
6. Cook on low heat, covered for approximately 1 hour stirring occasionally or till mung beans are thoroughly cooked.

# Mung Daal Soup

## Ingredients:

2 cups mung daal
1 teaspoon ginger/garlic masala
½ teaspoon green chillie masala
½ teaspoon turmeric powder
½ teaspoon red chillie powder
¾ teaspoon salt
3 tablespoons ghee
3 pieces cassia sticks
4 cloves
4 cups water

## Method:

1. Place washed mung daal in a deep pan with 4 cups of water. Cook daal on medium heat for 20 to 30 minutes or till daal is thoroughly cooked. To speed the process up cook daal in pressure cooker for 10 to 15 minutes.
2. Strain daal through a fine sieve in a dish. Add ginger/garlic masala, green chillie masala, red chillie powder, turmeric powder and salt.
3. Heat ghee in a pan and add cassia sticks and cloves. Add daal and stir. Cover and allow to cook on medium heat for 10 to 15 minutes till daal comes to a boil.

# Kadhee

## Ingredients:

½ cup chana flour
1 litre buttermilk
1 teaspoon garlic masala
½ teaspoon green chillie masala
¼ teaspoon red chillie powder
½ teaspoon turmeric powder
2 teaspoons crushed cumin
2 teaspoons salt
6 limeree leaves
2 teaspoons cumin seeds
2 tablespoons ghee
2 tablespoons chopped cilantro
2 cups water

## Method:

1. Mix chana flour with buttermilk in a large bowl.
2. Stir in garlic masala, green chillie masala, red chillie powder, turmeric powder, crushed cumin and salt.
3. In a deep saucepan melt 2 tablespoons of ghee on medium heat.
4. Add limeree leaves and whole cumin.
5. Add the buttermilk mixture and cover immediately. Keep covered for one minute to capture the flavors.
6. Add water and stir constantly till kadhee comes to full rolling boil.
7. Sprinkle with chopped cilantro.

Serve hot over a bed of basmati rice (see page 67).

# Indian Breads & Rices

# *Indian Breads & Rices*

# Roti (Chapatti)

## Ingredients:

1 cup all purpose flour
1 cup whole wheat flour
1 tablespoon ghee
½ teaspoon salt
1 - 2 cups hot water

## Method:

1. Combine all purpose flour, whole wheat flour, salt and ghee in a bowl. Work ghee into the flour until crumbly. Add only enough hot water to bind the dough.
2. Make 1 inch round balls and roll out into 4 to 6 inch rounds.
3. On a hot tawa cook roti lightly on one side for approximately 10 seconds. Turn roti over and cook for approximately 30 seconds. Turn the roti over again and cook until it puffs up.
4. Remove the roti and place it on a flat plate. Spread some ghee on the hot roti. Repeat steps 2 to 4, making a pile of the rotis, one on top of the other.
5. Serve roti with many of the spicy curries in this book.

# Naan

## Ingredients:

3 cups all purpose flour
4 tablespoons crushed cumin
1½ teaspoons salt
2 tablespoons fast active yeast
3 teaspoons sugar
4 tablespoons olive oil
1 to 2 cups hot water

## Method:

1. Mix flour, crushed cumin, salt, yeast, sugar and oil, till the flour is crumbly.
2. Use only enough hot water to bind the dough. Cover dough loosely with a plastic food wrap. Put the dough in a warm place and allow the dough to rise for about 2 hours.
3. Make 2 inch round balls with the dough. Roll into round shapes ¼ inch thick and cook on a hot tawa.
4. Place naan on tawa and allow to cook lightly on one side for approximately 10 seconds. Turn naan over again and cook until it puffs up.
5. Once the naan is puffed up or thoroughly cooked on both sides, remove and place on a flat plate. Butter both sides of the naan with butter or ghee.
6. Repeat steps 3 to 5, making a pile of the naan, one on top of the other.

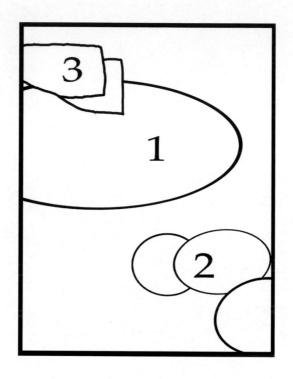

1. Chevtee Daal see page 55

2. Eggplant Papeta see page 21

3. Naan see page 64

# Baked Naan

## Ingredients:

4 cups all purpose flour
1 teaspoon baking powder
1 tablespoon fast active yeast
2 teaspoons sugar
1 teaspoon salt
¾ cup plain yogurt
1 egg beaten
2 tablespoons melted ghee
1 cup warm milk
4 tablespoons chopped cilantro
3 tablespoons crushed cumin

## Method:

1. Blend together flour, baking powder, salt, sugar, fast active yeast and melted ghee till flour is crumbly.
2. Make a well in the center and add yogurt, egg and milk. Fold in all the ingredients and knead the dough well.
3. Put in a warm place, covered loosely with a plastic food wrap and allow to rise for about 2 hours.
4. Roll out half the dough to approximately 10 inches by 6 inches wide. Place on a greased cookie sheet and bake in a preheated oven at 400°F, for 10 to 12 minutes or till golden brown.
5. Remove naan from the cookie sheet and spread butter lightly on top of the naan and sprinkle immediately with crushed cumin and chopped cilantro.
6. Cut naan into smaller segments and serve hot.

# Foolecha

## Ingredients:

3 cups all purpose flour
4 teaspoons crushed cumin
1½ teaspoons salt
2 tablespoons fast active yeast
3 teaspoons sugar
4 tablespoons olive oil
1-2 cups hot water
3 cups oil

## Method:

1. Mix flour, crushed cumin, salt, yeast, sugar and olive oil in a bowl till the flour is crumbly.
2. Use only enough hot water to bind the dough. Cover the dough loosely with plastic food wrap and put in a warm place. Allow the dough to rise for about 2 hours.
3. Take a handful of dough and roll out like a pizza shell, ¼ inch thick.
4. Cut dough with cookie cutters and deep fry in hot oil until foolechas puff up and are golden brown.
5. Remove from oil and drain in a colander. Serve hot or cold.

# Basmati Rice

## Ingredients:

1 cup basmati rice
1 teaspoon salt
2¼ cups water
1 tablespoon ghee

## Method:

1. Wash basmati rice about 3 times in warm water till water is clear.*
2. Cook rice in a pot with 2 cups of water on medium heat.
3. Add salt and stir.
4. Cook for about 10 to 15 minutes or till rice is half cooked.
5. Drain rice in a colander and set aside.
6. In the same pot add ½ teaspoon ghee to coat the bottom of the pot. Add the drained rice and ¼ cup of water. Spread the other ½ teaspoon ghee on the top of the rice and cover.
7. Allow the rice to cook on low heat for another 10 to 15 minutes or till rice is fully cooked.

*Basmati rice is a thin long grain. These grains are washed 3 times in warm water. The first wash will leave a milky water which is drained off. The second wash will be a lighter white colored water and the third wash usually leaves the water clear. This indicates the rice is clear of any white starch particles on the rice grains and therefore will not stick together when cooked.

# Yellow Rice with Onions

## Ingredients:

1 cup basmati rice
1 teaspoon salt
2¼ cups water
2 tablespoons ghee
½ onion finely sliced
1 teaspoon cumin seeds
½ teaspoon turmeric powder

## Method:

1. Wash rice 3 times in warm water till water is clear.
2. Cook rice in a pot with 2 cups water on medium heat.
3. Add salt and turmeric powder. Stir. Cook for 10 to 15 minutes or till rice is half cooked.
4. Drain rice in a colander and set aside. In the same pot heat 1½ tablespoons of ghee, cumin seeds and sliced onions. Sauté.
5. Add rice and stir. Add ¼ cup water and spread ½ tablespoon of ghee over the rice.
6. Cover and allow the rice to cook on low heat for 10 to 15 minutes or till rice is fully cooked.

# Ghee

## Ingredients:

**1 lb butter**

## Method:

1. Place butter in a saucepan on low heat.
2. Allow the butter to melt and come to a rolling boil.
3. Do not stir.  Continue boiling for 15 to 20 minutes or until the froth reduces considerably and you can see a clear yellow liquid.
4. Remove pan from the heat and allow ghee to cook down.
5. Sieve ghee through a thick layer of cheese cloth into a glass jar. Store ghee in cool dry place.

# Puri

## Ingredients:

2 cups all purpose flour
4 tablespoons olive oil
2 teaspoons salt
2 cups warm water
4 cups oil

## Method:

1. Mix flour, salt and olive oil in a bowl till flour is crumbly.
2. Bind dough with warm water to the consistency of a bread dough.
3. Take small amounts of dough and make ½ inch round balls.
4. Roll out each ball to about a 2 inch flat, round puri.
5. Heat oil in a deep fryer or wok on medium heat.
6. Fry puri in hot oil.  The puri will fluff up into a round ball.  Turn over the puri and remove when crispy golden brown.
7. Remove from oil and allow to cool in a colander.

# Condiments
# Masalas &
# Salads

# Condiments Masalas & Salads

# Apple Pickle

## Ingredients:

2 large cooking apples
1½ teaspoons red chillie powder
2 teaspoons salt
1 teaspoon turmeric powder
2 tablespoons olive oil

## Method:

1. In a bowl mix together red chillie powder, turmeric powder, salt and olive oil.
2. Wash and cut apples in small chunks.
3. Add apples to the chillie mixture and stir well.
4. Serve immediately.

# Raita

## Ingredients:

1 cucumber grated
3 teaspoons crushed cumin
2 garlic cloves grated
1 teaspoon salt
¼ teaspoon red chillie powder
¼ teaspoon mustard powder
4 tablespoons sour cream
¼ teaspoon turmeric powder
1 cup yogurt

## Method:

1. Grate cucumber in a bowl and sprinkle with ¼ teaspoon salt.  Stir.
2. Allow the cucumber to sit in a cool place for 5 minutes.
3. Take grated cucumber in both hands and squeeze the water out.
4.  Place the squeezed cucumber in a separate bowl and add crushed cumin, grated garlic, ¾ teaspoon salt, red chillie powder, mustard powder, sour cream, turmeric powder and yogurt.  Stir well.
5. Place raita in the fridge and serve cold.

# Katchoomber (Salad)

## Ingredients:

½ english cucumber
½ small onion
3 medium carrots
3 celery sticks
3 tablespoons olive oil
2 tablespoons cider vinegar
2 teaspoons salt
¼ teaspoon red chillie powder
1 teaspoon crushed cumin
2 tablespoons chopped cilantro

## Method:

1. Julianne cucumber, carrots and celery. Slice the onion finely and place all the vegetables in a large salad bowl.
2. Blend together olive oil, cider vinegar, salt, red chillie powder and crushed cumin.
3. Whisk vigorously and pour vinaigrette over salad. Toss just before serving.
4. Garnish with chopped cilantro.

# Cool Hot Cucumber Salad

## Ingredients:

1 english cucumber
1 teaspoon salt
1 teaspoon crushed cumin
¼ teaspoon green chillie masala

## Method:

1. Wash and cut cucumber into 2 inch long wedges.
2. Before serving add crushed cumin, salt and green chillie masala. Toss.

For a mild salad omit the green chillie masala.

# Cilantro Chutney

## Ingredients:

3 bunches cilantro or 3 cups cilantro
2 green chillies
3 garlic cloves
½ teaspoon pickling salt
3 teaspoons cumin seeds
juice of one lemon
½ teaspoon salt

## Method:

1. Wash and drain cilantro in a colander.
2. Process cilantro, green chillies, garlic cloves, cumin seeds and pickling salt in a chopper till the chutney is a smooth paste. Chutney can be placed in small sealed containers and placed in the freezer for future use.
3. Add lemon juice and salt just before serving.

# Tamarind Chutney

## Ingredients:

2 tablespoons tamarind paste
2 tablespoons finely chopped onions
1½ teaspoons red chillie powder
2 teaspoons salt
1 teaspoon ginger/garlic masala
½ teaspoon turmeric powder
3 teaspoons crushed cumin
¾ cup water
1 tablespoon chopped cilantro

## Method:

1. Mix together tamarind paste, onions, red chillie powder, turmeric powder, crushed cumin, ginger/garlic masala, salt and water.
2. Garnish with chopped cilantro.
3. Cover and place in the fridge before serving.

# Spicy Carrot Chutney

## Ingredients:

1 cup ketchup
4 tablespoons cider vinegar
2 garlic cloves grated
½ teaspoon red chillie powder
2 teaspoons crushed cumin
½ teaspoon mustard powder
1 teaspoon salt
¼ cup grated carrots
2 tablespoons unsweetened shredded coconut

## Method:

1. Mix  ketchup, cider vinegar, garlic, red chillie powder, crushed cumin, mustard powder, grated carrots, coconut and salt.
2. Serve cold.

# Notes

1. Chai (tea) see page 87
2. Raas Malai see page 90

# Great Spicy Tomato Sauce

## Ingredients:

1 cup tomato ketchup
4 tablespoons vinegar
2 garlic cloves grated
½ teaspoon red chillie powder
¼ teaspoon mustard powder
2 teaspoons crushed cumin
1 teaspoon salt

## Method:

1. In a bowl mix together garlic, red chillie powder, crushed cumin, mustard powder, salt and vinegar.
2. Add tomato ketchup and mix thoroughly.
3. Store in the fridge and serve cold.

Known as the "Great Sauce" in our household.

# Ginger/Garlic Masala

## Ingredients:

1 cup garlic cloves peeled
1 cup peeled ginger chopped
3 green chillies
¼ teaspoon pickling salt

## Method:

1. Place garlic, ginger, green chillies and salt in a chopper. Chop till masala is a fine paste.
2. Fill small sealed containers with masala and store in the freezer.

Frozen masalas will stay fresh in the freezer for up to a year. Ginger/ Garlic masala is used in many of the dishes in this cookbook.

# Green Chillie Masala

## Ingredients:

1 cup green chillies
¼ teaspoon pickling salt

## Method:

1. Wash and drain green chillies.
2. Place whole chillies and salt in a chopper.  Chop till masala looks like a paste.
3. Fill small sealed containers and store in the freezer.

Frozen masalas will stay fresh in the freezer for up to a year.  Green chillie masala is used in many of the dishes in this cookbook.  This is a very hot masala.  One can control the degree of hotness, by increasing or decreasing the amount of green chillie masala in the recipe.

# Garlic Masala

## Ingredients:

1 cup garlic cloves peeled
2 green chillies
¼ teaspoon pickling salt

## Method:

1. Peel garlic cloves and wash green chillies.
2. Place garlic, green chillies and salt in a chopper. Chop till masala is a fine paste.
3. Fill small sealed containers and store in the freezer.

Frozen masalas will stay fresh in the freezer for up to a year. Garlic masala is used mainly in fish dishes. A fun masala to use at your local Garlic Festivals to make garlic cookies, ice-cream, syrup etc.

# Desserts
# &
# Chai (Tea)

# Desserts
# &
# Chai (Tea)

# Chai (Tea)

## Ingredients:

3 cups water
1 inch piece ginger sliced
2 tea bags (black or orange pekoe)
¾ teaspoon chai masala
1 cup milk
sugar to taste

## Method:

1. Heat 3 cups of water in a saucepan with tea bags, sliced ginger and chai masala on medium heat.
2. Bring to boil and add 1 cup of milk.
3. Allow the mixture to come to a final boil and remove from heat.
4. Add sugar to taste when serving.

Chai is a very relaxing and soothing drink.  This is great on cold winter days or ski holidays. Chai is a soothing drink when you have a cold.  It opens up sinuses and the nasal passages.

# Cool Melon Dessert

## Ingredients:

½ seedless watermelon
½ cantaloupe
½ honeydew melon
1 cup green seedless grapes
1 cup red seedless grapes
4 tablespoons honey
juice of one lemon
4 tablespoons finely chopped mint

## Method:

1. Remove seeds from cantaloupe and honeydew melon.
2. Scoop out round balls of melon, using a melon baller, from all the melons and place in a large dessert dish.
3. Add washed green grapes and red grapes.
4. Mix honey, lemon juice and mint in a separate bowl.
5. Pour over all the fruit and toss.
6. Cover and place in a fridge.  Serve melon dessert cold.

A refreshing dessert to cool the palate after a delicious spicy meal.

# Jallebi

## Ingredients:

1 cup flour
1 tablespoon yogurt
1 teaspoon ghee
2 cups water
4 drops yellow food coloring
3 cups oil

Syrup:

2 cups sugar
1 cup water

## Method:

1. In a bowl stir in yogurt, ghee, 2 cups water, flour and food coloring to make a batter.
2. Make syrup by boiling sugar and water until all the sugar is dissolved. Remove from heat and set aside.
3. In a deep fryer or wok heat 3 cups of oil on medium heat.
4. Place the batter in an icing bag that has a small round tip on the end.
5. Make round swirls in the hot oil with the jallebi batter. Allow jallebi to cook till golden and crispy.
6. Remove jallebi and place immediately in the syrup.
7. Allow the syrup to seep into the jallebi for about 2 minutes. Remove jallebi and place on greaseproof paper and allow to cool.
8. Store jallebies in the fridge in a sealed container.

# Raas Malai

## Ingredients:

500g ricotta cheese
1¼ cups sugar
1½ litres half and half cream
1½ teaspoons ground cardamom
½ cup thinly sliced almonds
2 tablespoons coursely ground pistachio nuts

## Method:

1. Mix together ricotta cheese and ¼ cup of sugar.
2. Spread mixture on a cookie sheet and bake at 300ºF for 45 to 50 minutes.
3. Allow baked ricotta cheese to cool, then cut into small squares. Place squares in a large dessert dish.
4. In a large pot mix together half and half cream, 1 cup sugar and cardamom.
5. Heat mixture on medium heat stirring occasionally. Bring mixture to a rolling boil.
6. Pour the cream mixture over the ricotta cheese. Stir in almonds and pistachio nuts. Sprinkle ground cardamom to garnish.
7. Chill raas malai in the fridge.

Serve chilled in small dessert bowls.

# Nankatai (Shortbread)

## Ingredients:

¾ cups ghee
1 cup sugar
½ cup cream of wheat
1½ cups flour
1 teaspoon baking powder
½ cup milk
2 teaspoons ground cardamom

## Method:

1. Beat ghee and sugar till light and fluffy.
2. In a separate bowl mix together flour, cream of wheat, baking powder and 1 teaspoon ground cardamom.
3. Add flour mixture, a little at a time, to the wet mixture.
4. Add milk and mix thoroughly.
5. Make 1 inch round balls and place on a cookie sheet.
6. Sprinkle cookies with ground cardamom.
7. Bake in a preheated 375°F oven for 10 to 12 minutes.

Allow to cool and serve with chai (page 87).

# Kharkharya

## Ingredients:

4 cups all purpose flour
1 teaspoon salt
4 tablespoons ghee
½ cup sesame seeds

## Syrup:

1 cup sugar
$^2/_3$ cup water
1 tablespoon milk

## Method:

1. To make syrup heat water and sugar on medium heat.
2. Allow the syrup to come to boil and add milk.  Stir.
3. Remove from stove and set aside.  Allow syrup to cool until warm to the touch.
4. Mix flour, salt and ghee in a bowl till flour is crumbly.
5. Bind dough with syrup.  Make the dough the consistency of a bread dough.
6. Add sesame seeds and work into the dough.
7. Make 1 inch round balls and roll out with a velan into thin flat rounds of about 6 inches.
8. Fry kharkharya in hot oil till pastry is crispy  golden brown.
9. Store in a sealed container when cooled.

# Measurement Conversion Chart

| Temperature | |
| --- | --- |
| **Celsius (ºC)** | **Fahrenheit (ºF)** |
| 150ºC | 300ºF |
| 175ºC | 350ºF |
| 190ºC | 375ºF |
| 205ºC | 400ºF |
| 220ºC | 425ºF |

| Weight | |
| --- | --- |
| **Metric** | **Imperial** |
| 250g | ½ lb |
| 454g | 1 lb |
| 1 kg | 2.2 lb |
| 1.5 kg | 3 lb |
| 2.2 kg | 5 lb |

# Measurement Conversion Chart cont.

| Volume | |
|---|---|
| **Metric** | **Imperial** |
| 1 ml | ¼ teaspoon |
| 2 ml | ½ teaspoon |
| 5 ml | 1 teaspoon |
| 15 ml | 1 tablespoon |
| 60 ml | ¼ cup |
| 125 ml | ½ cup |
| 250 ml | 1 cup |

# Meal Suggestions

## Meal 1

Chicken Curry (page 29) or Butter Chicken (page 27)
Spicy Corn with Red Peppers (page 49)
Basmati Rice (page 67)
Naan (page 64) or Roti (page 63)
Spicy Tomato Sauce (page 81) or Cilantro Chutney (page 77)
Cool Melon Dessert (page 88)
Chai (page 87)

## Meal 2

Pakodas (page 19)
Spicy Baked Pepper Chicken (page28)
Ginger/Garlic Potatoes (page 50)
Naan (page 64)
Cool Hot Cucumber Salad (page 76)
Spicy Carrot Chutney (page 79)
Cool Melon Dessert (page 88)
Chai (page 87)

# Meal Suggestions

## Meal 3

Spicy Meat Ball Curry (page 39)
Yellow Rice with Onions (page 68)
Spicy Pepper and Potato dish (page 48)
Katchoomber (page 75)
Cilantro Chutney (page 77)
Cool Melon Dessert (page 88)
Chai (page 87)

## Meal 4

Shrimp Curry (page 36)
Cauliflower Potato Curry (page 43)
Baked Naan (page 65)
Basmati Rice (page 67)
Cool Hot Cucumber Salad (page 76)
Cilantro Chutney (page 77)
Cool Melon Dessert (page 88)
Chai (page 87)

# Meal Suggestions

## Meal 5

Spicy Beef Stirfry (page 34)
Basmati Rice (page 67)
Katchoomber (page 75)
Apple Pickle (page 73)
Raas Malai (page 90)
Chai (page 87)

## Meal 6

Okra Curry (page 46)
Spinach Curry (page 44)
Kadee (page 60)
Basmati Rice (page 67)
Raita (page 74)
Raas Malai (page 90)
Chai (page 87)

# Meal Suggestions

## Meal 7

Raveya (page 47)
Vadhu (page 58)
Roti (page 63) or Puri (page 70)
Katchoomber (page 75)
Apple Pickle (page 73)
Jallebi (page 89) or Raas Malai (page 90)
Chai (page 87)

## Meal 8

Pakodas (page 19) or Samosas (page 13)
Eggplant Potato Curry (page 45)
Basmati Rice (page 67)
Cool Hot Cucumber Salad (page 76)
Tamarind Chutney (page 78)
Nankatai (page 91) or Raas Malai (page 90)
Chai (page 87)

# Meal Suggestions

## Meal 9

Eggplant Papeta (page 21)
Chevtee Daal (page 55)
Roti (page 63)
Katchoomber (page 75)
Apple Pickle (page 73)
Raas Malai (page 90)
Chai (page 87)

## Meal 10

Mung Daal Soup (page 59)
Okra Curry (page 46)
Roti (page 63)
Raita (page 74)
Raas Malai (page 90)
Chai (page 87)

These are only a few suggestions for you to try. Some of the dishes in this book are meals in themselves. Happy Cooking!

# Glossary

All spices, spice blends and cookware needed for Indian cooking, mentioned in this glossary are available at, *Daksha's Gourmet Spices* order over the internet at, *www.spicesgourmet.com*

## Ba's Biryani
Biryani is a multi layered dish consisting of meat curry, rice and yogurt. Ba means mother in the Gujarati language.

## Basmati Rice
This is a thin long grain rice, grown on the foothills of the Himalayas.

## Black mustard seed
Seeds of the mustard plant.

## Cassia sticks
The outer bark of a cinnamon tree.

## Chai Masala
Daksha's own blend of spices used with tea to make a delicious soothing drink. The word chai means tea.

## Chana flour
A lentil flour made out of chana daal.

## Chevtee daal
A mixture of daals, for example, toower daal mixed with urad daal (see daal on page 101).

## Chutney
A blended condiment made with vegetables and spices.

## Cilantro
Also known as Chinese parsley. A fresh tasting herb grown by planting coriander seeds.

## Cumin
A seed commonly used in Gujarati cooking.

## Daal
A split bean without the husk, for example urad daal, mung daal, toower daal and chana daal.

## Foolecha
Little round fried bread made with spices, flour and yeast.

## Garam Masala
Garam means warm. A mixture of Daksha's own blends of spices used mainly in meat dishes.

## Ghee
Clarified butter.

## Jallebi
A crispy sweet yellow dessert in the shape of round swirls.

## Julienne
To cut into long thin strips.

## Katchoomber
A crunchy salad made with spices.

## Kharkharya
A crispy sweet, deep fried dessert.

## Limeree Leaves
Also known as curry leaves.

## Marinate
To tenderize and flavor foods by covering in spice mixtures.

## Masala
Masala means mixture.

## Nankatai
An Indian shortbread.

## Pakoras
A deep fried vegetable appetizer made with a lentil flour.

## Pilaf
A spicy rice dish combined with meat or vegetables.

## Puri
Little round shaped fried bread, made with flour.

## Raas Malai
A dessert made with fresh cream, nuts and cardamom.

## Raita
Spicy cucumber condiment.

## Raveya
Stuffed, cooked vegetables, for example stuffed eggplant.

## Red chillie powder
Made from hot chillie peppers that have been dried and ground. Red chillie pepper is very potent, so be sure not to touch your eyes while cooking with it.

## Roti

A flat bread made with wheat flour.

## Saffron

A highly expensive, orange-red spice made from the stigmas of a crocus flower.

## Stir fry

To fry sliced food quickly over medium to high heat in a pan or wok.

## Tapeli

A curry dish made with very little sauce.

## Tawa

A traditional Indian pan made specially to cook rotis and naan bread. It is a concave pan with no edges. A non-stick frying pan may be used instead of a tawa.

## Thana Jeeroo

Daksha's own blend of spices used in both meat and vegetable dishes.

## Turmeric powder

Turmeric roots are dried thoroughly, then ground to make a fine powder.

## Vadhu

A spicy dish made with sprouted beans.

## Vagarela

To stir fry in flavored oil.

## Velan

A traditional Indian rolling pin used for making rotis, naan and puris. A conventional rolling pin may be used instead of a velan.

# Index

# Index

# Index

# Index

# Notes

# Notes

# Notes

www.spicesgourmet.com

# Notes

www.spicesgourmet.com

www.spicesgourmet.com

# Daksha's Gourmet Spices

# Cookbook II

# Happy Cooking!

## Daksha Narsing
## www.spicesgourmet.com

 Daksha's Gourmet Spices

First print 2002
Reprint 2003
Reprint 2004
Reprint 2005
Reprint 2007

Written by Daksha Narsing
Cover Design & Layout by Amesh Narsing
Photography by Tracey Kusiewicz

ISBN 0-9681253-2-8

Distributed by:   Daksha's Gourmet Spices
                  Williams Lake, B.C., Canada
                  V2G 3T9

Daksha's spices and cookware may be purchased at:
**www.spicesgourmet.com**
E-mail: daksha@telus.net

Published by:  APS Publishers
Printed in Canada by: Friesens

Daksha's Gourmet Spices